CONTENTS

4

How do my senses work?

Mike Jackson

Illustrated by Jon Davis

First published in this edition in 2011 by
Evans Publishing Group
2A Portman Mansions
Chiltern Street
London W1U 6NR

© Evans Brothers Limited 2011

www.evansbooks.co.uk

British Library Cataloguing in Publication Data
A CIP catalogue record for this book is available from the British Library

ISBN: 9780237544935

Planned and produced by Discovery Books
Cover designed by Rebecca Fox

For permission to reproduce copyright material the author and publishers gratefully acknowledge the following: Bruce Coleman: (Kim Taylor) page 9; Greg Evans: page 11; Image Bank: Page 19 (right); istock: cover, page 15; Last Resort Picture Library; page 25; Popperfoto: page 17; Alex Ramsay: pages 12, 17; Tony Stone Worldwide: page 19 (bottom)

Printed by Great Wall Printing Company in Chai Wan, Hong Kong, August 2011, Job Number 1672.

We use our eyes to see things all around us. Sight is one of our senses.

We use our noses to smell things like food or flowers. Smell is another of our senses.

8

We use our ears to hear the world around us. Hearing is also one of our senses.

10

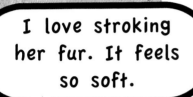

We use our fingers to touch things. Touch is one of our senses.

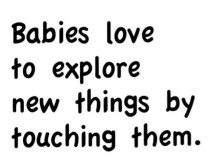

Babies love to explore new things by touching them.

We use our tongue to taste the foods that we eat. Taste is our fifth sense. We have five senses altogether.

Some people wear glasses to help them to see clearly.

If you find it hard to see things that are far away, you are short-sighted. If objects that are nearby seem blurred, you are long-sighted.

Some things taste sweet and some things taste sour. Fruits like pineapples are very sweet, but lemons can be very sour!

Some things feel hot and some things feel cold. We can feel things with the nerves all over our bodies.

You can often tell if food is hot because it is steaming. Don't touch!

We like the smell of some things.
We don't like the smell of other
things. What do you like the
smell of?

If we listen carefully, we can hear quiet noises.

23

Some noises are really loud!

We have five senses. They are sight, smell, hearing, touch and taste.

We use our senses to enjoy the world around us.

Fun activities

Each of these pictures shows a different sense. Can you work out which sense is in each picture?

Shut your eyes — what can you hear?

When you concentrate on listening carefully, it's surprising how much you can hear. Are there birds singing or dogs barking? Can you hear traffic noises or people talking? Is there any music playing? Write down everything that you can hear.

Imagine that you are going for a walk by the seaside.

Write an account of your walk, paying special attention to the experiences of all five senses. What would you be able to see and hear? Does the seaside have a particular smell? Describe things that you might touch, and how they feel, for example sand, pebbles, seaweed or shells. What might you touch on your walk? What sort of things do you like to eat at the seaside, and how do they taste?

Interesting websites:

A fun, interactive website exploring how our eyes work:
http://www.bootslearningstore.com/ks2/eyesight.html

Some experiments that use our senses, which you can try at home:
http://kidshealth.org/kid/closet/experiments/
experiment_main.html

Learn all about your senses of taste and smell:
http://www.childrensuniversity.manchester.ac.uk/interactives/
science/brainandsenses/taste.asp

Index